Aggravated assault on Paul Pelosi:
The man who accepted a beating in place of his wife.

by Sharon Benjamin.

Table of contents

Chapter 1: All we need to know about the man.

Paul Pelosi was born and nurtured in San Francisco, the youngest in a family of three sons.

His father was John Pelosi, a wholesale pharmacist. He attended St. Ignatius High School and graduated from Malvern Preparatory School in Pennsylvania. He got a bachelor of science (BS) in foreign service at Georgetown University, during which he met his future wife, Nancy D'Alesandro, who was attending a Roman Catholic women's institution, Trinity College, in Washington, D.C. He obtained an MBA from the Stern School of Business at New York University. He has been the head of the Foreign Service Board at Georgetown since 2009.

Pelosi created and leads the venture capital business Financial Leasing Services, Inc., through which he and his wife have a personal wealth of around $114 million.

Having previously invested in the Oakland Invaders of the United States Football League, he acquired the California Redwoods, a franchise in the United Football League, for $12 million in 2009. The Redwoods then relocated to Sacramento to become the Sacramento Mountain Lions.

Pelosi's skill in stock trading garnered public attention in the summer of 2021, leading to measures to rigorously limit individual stock ownership by members of Congress.

Pelosi married Nancy Pelosi (née D'Alesandro), on September 7, 1963, at the Cathedral of Mary Our Queen in Baltimore, Maryland. They have five children. Nancy became the 52nd Speaker of the U.S. House of Representatives in 2007.

In May 2022, Pelosi was detained for driving under the influence of alcohol in Napa County when he slammed with another at an intersection. Pelosi pleaded guilty in August 2022 and was sentenced to serve five days in prison, paying $6,800 in penalties and reparations, completing a DUI program, as well as three years of probation.

Chapter 2: The horrific assault.

Paul Pelosi, the husband of House Speaker Nancy Pelosi, was struck with a hammer at the couple's home in San Francisco by a male attacker early Friday morning. The attacker who assaulted him was seeking the speaker of the House, according to a person informed on the incident.

The invader accosted the speaker's husband in their San Francisco home yelling, "Where is Nancy? Where is Nancy?" according to the source. The guy who attacked Paul Pelosi wanted to tie him up "until Nancy arrived home," according to two persons familiar with the case. When the cops came, the attacker was stating he was "waiting for Nancy."

Pelosi, 82, was brought to a hospital and had a "successful operation to heal a skull fracture and major damage to his right arm and hands," Drew Hammill, a spokesperson for Nancy Pelosi, said in a statement early Friday evening. The statement claimed that physicians anticipate he will make a complete recovery.

Authorities are still identifying a motive in the assault, but they aim to file the man on felony charges.

The incident sent shockwaves through Washington and triggered an outpouring of sympathy and outrage from congressional leaders on both sides of the aisle. It comes as worries of political violence intended at politicians remain high in the wake of January 6, 2021, assault on the US Capitol as well as other high-profile violent events that have targeted members of Congress in previous years.

Nancy Pelosi was able to talk to her husband after the incident and before he was rushed into surgery, according to a person familiar with the issue. The speaker went with her family to San Francisco on Friday to be with her husband, and another person knowledgeable with CNN Friday evening that she was at the hospital.

Authorities identified 42-year-old David DePape as the suspect in the attack. Officials aim to "bring forth several criminal charges" in connection with the incident next week, San Francisco District Attorney Brooke Jenkins tweeted Friday evening.

"We are collaborating closely with federal and local law enforcement partners on this inquiry. We will bring up additional felony charges on Monday and anticipate DePape to be arraigned on Tuesday. DePape will be held responsible for his horrific crimes," she added.

Detailed details from Friday evening of what responding law enforcement personnel observed when they got to the location;

When cops arrived at the Pelosi house, the front door was unlocked "by someone inside," and the officers — from outside the door – witnessed Pelosi and DePape each having a hand "on a single hammer."

While remaining outside the residence, cops watched DePape yank the hammer away from Pelosi and strike Pelosi, the police chief said. Inside sources suggest that Pelosi was hit by DePape at least once.

The cops promptly grabbed the offender, disarmed him, put him into custody, called emergency assistance, and gave medical aid," states law enforcement.

Paul Pelosi was able to contact 911 at the onset of the assault, according to a law enforcement source and another person familiar with the situation. He managed to keep the line open and the dispatcher could hear the dialogue in the background, according to the law enforcement source.

Pelosi was talking in code, claimed the law enforcement source, offering enough information so that the operator overhearing it might tell that there was something amiss. At the same time, Pelosi appeared to be attempting not to make it plain to the intruder that he had an open line, the insider stated.

The source stated the dispatcher could hear Pelosi chatting about what was going on and called the police to check on the residence.

The battle with Pelosi was filmed on a police body camera when cops burst through the door to intercede, according to one of the sources.

Police have been able to talk with the suspect, who received "some minor injuries" during the incident,

The guy who reportedly assaulted Paul Pelosi early Friday shared memes and conspiracy theories on Facebook regarding Covid vaccinations, the 2020 election, and the January 6 attack, and an acquaintance told CNN that he appeared "out of touch with reality."

DePape was not known to US Capitol Police and was not in any government databases monitoring threats, according to three people who were informed of the inquiry.

The US Capitol Police announced in a statement earlier in the morning that they are aiding the FBI and the San Francisco Police "with a collaborative investigation" into the break-in at the Pelosi house in California.

The perpetrator entered the Pelosi property from the rear of the house, according to two persons acquainted with the early circumstances of the event.

With Speaker Pelosi traveling, there would not have been a security detail at the mansion, according to one person familiar with the procedure.

There may be footage that US Capitol Police and law enforcement may analyze since there are security cameras at the property, according to two law enforcement sources.

Chapter 3: What we know about the assailant.

Childhood in Canada. A stint on the Big Island of Hawaii. Relocation to the Bay Area. A stretch of pro-nudity advocacy.
And then, most lately, an apparent fascination with putting right-wing conspiracy theories onto the internet – spending hours and days in front of a computer, populating online sites that had no apparent audience.
This was the strange and peripatetic life of 42-year-old David DePape before he was accused of breaking into the San Francisco home of Democratic House Speaker Nancy Pelosi and striking her husband, Paul Pelosi, with a hammer, leaving him in need of surgeries to repair a fractured skull and injuries to his right arm and hands.

The guy suspected of beating Paul Pelosi with a hammer sexually tortured his kids and stepdaughter as youngsters, one of the alleged victims said in online remarks.

David DePape, 42, was "consumed with darkness," Inti Gonzalez accused on Facebook and in a blog post.

"This assault on Nancy Pelosi's husband came as a shock to me, but not much given the type of horrific torture he had perpetrated on me and my brothers," the 20-something Gonzalez wrote.

Gonzalez characterized DePape as someone who "did want to be a decent person," but added, "the monster in him was always too big for him to be safe to be around."

Paul Pelosi attacker David DePape lived on a school bus

In the months before police accused him of beating House Speaker Nancy Pelosi's husband Friday morning, David DePape had been slipping more into the realm of far-right conspiracies, antisemitism, and hatred, according to a Times analysis of his online profiles.

In a personal blog that DePape kept, articles cover such themes as "Manipulation of History," "Holohoax" and "It's OK to be white." He referenced 4chan, a popular messaging board of the extreme right. He uploaded films alleging conspiracies including COVID-19 vaccinations and the conflict in Ukraine being a plot for Jewish people to purchase the property.

DePape's screeds included writings about QAnon, an unproven belief that former President Trump is at war with a conspiracy of Satan-worshipping elites who operate a child sex ring and govern the globe. In an Aug. 23 article headed "Q," DePape wrote: "Either Q is Trump himself or Q is the deep state moles inside Trump's close circle."

DePape's daughter, Inti Gonzalez, informed The Times that her father published the blog. She added that she and her mother were reeling from the news that DePape had been detained in connection with the assault on Paul Pelosi.

Chapter 4: The blame game Subliminals begin.

President Joe Biden on Friday condemned the "despicable" attack on House Speaker Nancy Pelosi's husband, Paul, explicitly linked the attacker's statements to rioters' slogans during the Jan. 6 assault on the Capitol.

There are reports "that the same chant was used by this guy that they have in custody that was used on January 6, the attack on the U.S. Capitol," Biden said during an impassioned speech at the annual Pennsylvania Democratic Party's Independence Dinner, where he and Vice President Kamala Harris were campaigning for Pennsylvania's Democratic nominees.

The perpetrator's demands of "Where's Nancy?" during the house invasion early Friday morning mimicked the slogans of pro-Trump protesters who scoured the Capitol's hallways for the speaker to derail the certification of Biden's 2020 win.

"This is disgusting. There's no place in America. There's too much violence — political violence — too much anger, too much vitriol," Biden remarked. "And what makes us believe one party can speak about stolen elections, Covid being a fraud, that it's all a bunch of falsehoods, and it does not affect those who may not be so well balanced? What makes us assume that it's not going to impact the political climate? Enough is enough is enough."

Biden launched his remarks urging the gathering to take a quick moment to "send our love to Nancy Pelosi," adding that he had talked to the speaker and her husband "seems to be getting along well." He then urged "every person of good conscience" to "clearly and unmistakably speak out against the violence in our politics, regardless of what your views are."

Earlier Friday, Harris blamed the present political atmosphere for motivating the assault, calling it "an act of terrible violence."

"I believe we're looking at a period in our nation when there is so much conversation that is fuelled by hatred and division," Harris told reporters, "and anybody who purports to be a leader needs to fully grasp the meaning and the effect of their words and their stance on matters like this."

Donald Trump Jr. remarked on the recent house burglary and assault on Paul Pelosi, the husband of House Speaker Nancy Pelosi, saying it should encourage Democrats to confront violent crime more seriously.

In a post on Truth Social Saturday afternoon, the former president's son accused Democratic politicians of not doing more to aid common residents, considering their broad response to Friday's break-in.

"Imagine how safe the nation would be if democrats took all violent crime as seriously as they're treating the Paul Pelosi case," Trump Jr. posted to his 2.6 million followers on the app.

"They just don't care about you," he continued in the article.

Chapter 5: My small .viewpointt

An assailant stormed into the California home of House Speaker Nancy Pelosi early Friday and struck her husband Paul Pelosi with a hammer while she was in Washington, DC.

This terrible occurrence is only the latest in a series of growing assaults and confrontations against politicians, and women politicians in particular - many of whom endure outrageous hostility on the Internet that crosses over into actual threats or violence. Social media networks and law enforcement must act immediately to halt this abuse before a politician is seriously hurt or murdered.

From 2017 to 2021, threats against members of Congress investigated by US Capitol Police surged by 144%, Axios found. Many of the parliamentarians on the receiving end of these threats are women and people of color.

After an intruder destroyed a glass in the house of Republican Sen. Susan Collins, she told The New York Times, "What began with unpleasant phone calls is now translating into actual threats of violence and real violence." She stated, "I wouldn't be astonished if a senator or House member were killed."

Democratic Rep. Pramila Jayapal has been harassed by a guy who showed up regularly outside her house, loaded with a weapon. Jayapal's husband stated he heard the sounds of two guys yelling obscenities and saying that they would stop pestering her area if she killed herself.

Frustrated MPs seek safety for their families as threats mount
"We sign up for a lot of things when we join up for this job," Jayapal told the Times. "But

having someone go up to your door with a pistol, terrifying your neighbors, worrying your employees, and attempting to intimidate me — it's impossible to describe."

Last year, Republican Rep. Nancy Mace of South Carolina alleged her house was assaulted with vulgar graffiti.
And Democratic Rep. Alexandria Ocasio-Cortez of New York gets so many threats that she has a round-the-clock security staff and, at times, sleeps in various places. Her colleague, Republican Rep. Paul Gosar of Arizona, posted an edited anime video of himself pretending to assassinate her last year. (Gosar erased the video and did not apologize. An hour after the House decided to rebuke him and remove him from two committee assignments last year, he retweeted a post that featured the video.)

Gosar's video — and the deluge of hate Ocasio-Cortez has received in its aftermath — highlights how internet harassment can make the world less secure for women. As I've stated previously, evidence reveals that viewing violence in the media is connected with performing acts of violence or aggressiveness.

Toxic, widely-tolerated social media material is helping normalize assaults on women who lead — which might help explain why women like Pelosi are suddenly becoming the subject of actual violence.

Pelosi is a particular focus of vitriol among the right. In 2019, the House Speaker, who has frequently fought with Former President Donald Trump, became the target of edited recordings that made her look as if she were tripping over and slurring her words. Those films were then pushed by Donald Trump and his lawyer Rudy Giuliani on social media, where they became viral. During the January 6 raid on the Capitol last year, Trump fans destroyed her office and cried,

"Where are you, Nancy?" – a terrifying echo of the words DePape said on Friday: "Where is Nancy?"

The harassment, bigotry, and violence must cease.

Social media corporations say they don't accept this type of hatred. Yet the fact is clear: it continues to exist on their platforms. They must become serious about employing algorithms and human moderators to take down this abuse. Any time consumers encounter online hatred like Gosar's video, we should quickly utilize accessible reporting methods so these social networks can take it down.

Of course, it's sobering that this attack on Pelosi happened just as Elon Musk finalized his purchase of Twitter, given that Musk has indicated that he favors more lenient content moderation policies. If Twitter – or any other site – becomes a greater quagmire of sexism and harassment, then users should make the option to cease using it.

The FBI should also investigate and punish the abuse of women both online and off. If the agency requires additional cash to achieve it, Congress could charge a tax on social networks to support an increase in resources. I assume the many politicians who have been intimidated and harassed would be pleased to cast a vote in support of such a measure.

The unprecedented assault on the Pelosi house demonstrates how violence against members of Congress is getting out of control. It's time for social media firms to stop publishing information that normalizes this sort of violence and for the FBI to get serious about investigating and prosecuting these crimes. They should take this tragic tragedy as the wake-up call that it is, and not wait for Sen. Collins' forecast that a member of Congress may end up dead to come true.